# Where Does the Hen Lay Her Eggs?

By
Amanda Hansen

Copyright © 2018 by Amanda J. Hansen
All rights reserved.

Where Does the Hen Lay Her Eggs?

No part of this book may be reproduced or utilized in any form or by any means, electronic, digital, audio or photocopying, without the expressed written consent of the author.

ISBN- 13: 978-1-7325161-1-3

ISBN- 10: 1-7325161-1-1

I Want to Thank

My husband Paul, who encourages me every day to keep writing and follow my dreams.

My sons Eric and Jonathon, and my daughter-in-law Andrea, who are my biggest cheerleaders.

My grandchildren Adelyn and Garrett; and my dad, who keeps telling me to write my books.

Thank you, Kathryn Holt, for your time you commit to me.

My friends for their love and support; and my students, who inspire me with their imaginations every day.

Where does the hen lay her eggs?

Do you ever think to yourself, I wonder where a hen lays all of her eggs?

Get ready to go on an adventure around Hansen's Farm. Hansen's Farm is located in Havre, along the Hi-Line of North Central Montana.

Does the hen lay her eggs on the bird bath?

Does the hen lay her eggs by the duck pond?

Does the hen lay her eggs inside the water fountain?

Does the hen lay her eggs in the goat house?

Does the hen lay her eggs beneath the bird feeder?

Does the hen lay her eggs under the bushes?

Does the hen lay her eggs inside the donkey feeder?

Does the hen lay her eggs behind the duck feeder?

Does the hen lay her eggs on the bench?

Does the hen lay her eggs in the flower pot?

Does the hen lay her eggs in the hay pile?

Does the hen lay her eggs inside the flower basket?

Does the hen lay her eggs beside the rock?

Does the hen lay her eggs in the mailbox?

Does the hen lay her eggs on top of the milk can?

Does the hen lay her eggs in the tree?

Does the hen lay her eggs inside the wishing well?

Does the hen lay her eggs in the wood pile?

Does the hen lay her eggs inside the peacock house?

Does the hen lay her eggs by the hen house?

Oh, here is the hen. Where are her eggs?

The hen lays her eggs inside her nest box.

www.ingramcontent.com/pod-product-compliance
Lightning Source LLC
Chambersburg PA
CBHW042122040426
42450CB00002B/38